Contents

Head, Shoulders, Knees, and Toes

Song

Head, shoulders, knees, and toes,
Knees and toes,
Knees and toes.
Head, shoulders, knees, and toes,
Eyes and ears and mouth and
nose.

Clucky, the Unlucky Ducky
Play

Characters

 Storyteller
(teacher or other fluent reader)

 Clucky Ducky

Other Ducklings
(any number)

Storyteller:
One day Clucky Ducky went for a walk and she slipped over in the mucky mucky mud! The other little ducklings said:

Other Ducklings:
Poor Clucky Ducky. You are an unlucky little duck.

Storyteller:
Then she slid down the slimy, slimy hill. The other little ducklings said:

Other Ducklings:
Poor Clucky Ducky. You are an unlucky little duck.

Storyteller:
Then she splashed into the cold, cold water. The other little ducklings said:

Other Ducklings:
Poor Clucky Ducky. You are an unlucky little duck.

Storyteller:
Then the farmer pulled her out of the cold, cold water, warmed her in front of the warm, warm fire and gave her some tasty, tasty wheat to eat.
Little Clucky Ducky smiled and said:

Clucky Ducky:
I am a lucky clucky ducky. I am a lucky, lucky duck. I am a lucky clucky ducky.

3

Grumpy Bumper Boat

Poem

I'm a Grumpy Bumper Boat.

You can bump tugboats. You can bump rocks.

You can bump octopuses sitting knitting socks.

You can bump yellow yachts sailing on the sea.

But I'm a grumpy bumper boat, so don't bump me!

One Potato, Two Potato

Counting Rhyme

One potato,

two potato,

three potato,

four.

Five potato,

six potato,

seven potato,

more.

Boing! Up! Woof! Down!

Rhyme

Boing! Up! Woof! Down!

Boing! Up! Woof! Down!

Boing! Up! Woof! Meeeeeoww!!

The dog was on the trampoline,

The cat's on now!

The Great Gorilla Football Game

Play

 Field Announcer:
Good afternoon, Gorillas! Welcome to the game!
Who is the home team? What is their name?

 Green Gorillas Fans:
Green Gorillas!
Green Gorillas!
Go! Go! Go!
Have you seen a better team?
No! No! No!

 GREEN GORILLAS, GO! GO! GO!

 Field Announcer:
First down, second down, third down, four!
A Gorilla gets a touchdown! The Green Gorillas score!

 Green Gorillas Fans:
Green Gorillas!
Green Gorillas!
Go! Go! Go!
Have you seen a better team?
No! No! No!

 Field Announcer:
The referee blows the whistle at the end of the game.
Who made the touchdown? What is their name?

 Green Gorillas Fans:
Green Gorillas!
Green Gorillas!
Go! Go! Go!
Have you seen a better team?
No! No! No!

If You're Happy And You Know It

Song

If you're happy and you know it, clap your hands. *(clap, clap)*

If you're happy and you know it, clap your hands. *(clap, clap)*

If you're happy and you know it,

Then you really ought to show it.

If you're happy and you know it, clap your hands. *(clap, clap)*

If you're sleepy and you know it, nod your head. *(nod, nod)*

If you're sleepy and you know it, nod your head. *(nod, nod)*

If you're sleepy and you know it,

Then you really ought to show it.

If you're sleepy and you know it, nod your head. *(nod, nod)*

Humpty Dumpty

Nursery Rhyme

Humpty Dumpty sat on a wall,

Humpty Dumpty had a great fall.

All the king's horses

And all the king's men

Couldn't put Humpty together again.

I Wiggle My Fingers

Rhyme

I wiggle my fingers,

I wiggle my toes,

I wiggle my shoulders,

I wiggle my nose.

Now no more wiggles are left in me,

So I will be still, as still as can be.

Teddy Bear, Teddy Bear

Rhyme

Teddy Bear, Teddy Bear, turn around.

Teddy Bear, Teddy Bear, touch the ground.

Teddy Bear, Teddy Bear, show your shoe.

Teddy Bear, Teddy Bear, please skiddoo!

11

Blue Budgie

Play

 Storyteller: One day, the blue budgie flew to the mat where the dog was sleeping. The dog looked up and said:

 Dog: Where are you going, blue budgie, blue budgie? Where are you going, blue budgie so blue?

 Storyteller: And the blue budgie said:

 Blue Budgie: I'm going to fly to the top of the sky to show what a budgie can do.

 Storyteller: Then the blue budgie flew up onto the chair where the cat was sleeping. The cat woke up and said:

 Cat: Where are you going, blue budgie, blue budgie? Where are you going, blue budgie so blue?

Storyteller: And the blue budgie said:

 Blue Budgie: I'm going to fly to the top of the sky to show what a budgie can do.

 Storyteller: Then the blue budgie flew up onto the shelf where the goldfish was swimming in the bowl. The goldfish looked up and said:

 Goldfish: Where are you going, blue budgie, blue budgie? Where are you going, blue budgie so blue?

 Storyteller: And the blue budgie said:

 Blue Budgie: I'm going to fly to the top of the sky to show what a budgie can do.

 Storyteller: Then the blue budgie flew up, up, and up some more! The blue budgie flew so high that she bumped her head on the ceiling! The cat, the dog, and the goldfish all looked at her and said:

Cat, Dog, and Goldfish: What are you doing, blue budgie, blue budgie; little blue budgie so blue?

 Storyteller: And the blue budgie rubbed her head with her wing and said:

 Blue Budgie: I'm going to sit on my perch for a bit, now you know what a budgie can do.

 Good and Bad

Play

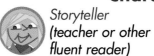
Storyteller: One day Cindy was sailing to school in a big ship.

Everyone: That's good!

Storyteller: No, that's bad. The ship got stuck on the rocks.

Everyone: That's bad!

Storyteller: No, that's good. A big tractor came to pull the ship off the rocks.

Everyone: That's good!

Storyteller: No, that's bad. The tractor's wheels got stuck in the mud.

Everyone: That's bad!

Storyteller: No, that's good. A big bulldozer came to push the tractor out of the mud.

Everyone: That's good!

Storyteller: No, that's bad. The bulldozer got stuck in the sand.

Everyone: That's bad!

Storyteller: No, that's good. A big crane came to lift the bulldozer out of the sand.

Everyone: That's good!

Storyteller: No, that's bad. The crane lifted the bulldozer and Cindy high into the sky and then the wire broke.

Everyone: That's bad!

Storyteller: No, that's good. Cindy fell onto the wing of a big plane.

Everyone: That's good!

Storyteller: No, that's bad. Cindy fell off the wing.

Everyone: That's bad!

Storyteller: No, that's good. Cindy fell into a big truck full of feathers and it took her to school.

Everyone: That's good!

Storyteller: No, that's bad. It was Saturday and the school was closed.

Everyone: That's bad! That's very, very bad!

Lemonade

Rhyme

Lemonade, crunchy ice,

Beat it once, beat it twice.

Lemonade, crunchy ice,

Beat it once, beat it twice.

Turn around, touch the ground,

FREEZE.

Where Would You Like to Live?
Play

 Leader: Would you like to live in an old tin can?

 Followers: No, we wouldn't like to live in an old tin can!

 Leader: Would you like to live in an old tin can with a bike in the bath and a pizza in the pan?

 Followers: No, we wouldn't like to live in an old tin can with a bike in the bath and a pizza in the pan!

 Leader: Would you like to live in an old shoe box?

 Followers: No, we wouldn't like to live in an old shoe box!

Leader: Would you like to live in an old shoe box with a flower in the shower and a fridge full of socks?

 Followers: No, we wouldn't like to live in an old shoe box with a flower in the shower and a fridge full of socks!

 Leader: Would you like to live in a big blue sack?

 Followers: No, we wouldn't like to live in a big blue sack!

 Leader: Would you like to live in a big blue sack with a kitten in the kitchen and a tiger out the back?

 Followers: No, we wouldn't like to live in a big blue sack with a kitten in the kitchen and a tiger out the back!

 Leader: Would you like to live in a rabbit hutch?

 Followers: No, we wouldn't like to live in a rabbit hutch!

 Leader: Would you like to live in a rabbit hutch or would you rather live at your place, thank you very much?

 Followers: No, we wouldn't like to live in a rabbit hutch, we'd rather live at our place, thank you very much!

Sam, the Skateboard Snail

Poem

I go past the motorcycles.
I go past the cars.
I go past the rocket ships,
Zooming to the stars.

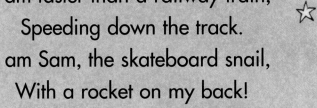

I am faster than a railway train,
Speeding down the track.
I am Sam, the skateboard snail,
With a rocket on my back!

We Are the Flag

Play

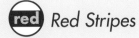 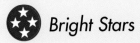
 Red Stripes: We are the red stripes, bright and long!

 White Stripes: We are the white stripes, pure and strong!

 Bright Stars: We are the bright stars, shining on the blue!

Everyone: We are the flag that flies over you.

 Red Stripes: We fly on flagpoles.

 White Stripes: We fly on trains.

 Bright Stars: We fly on buildings.

Everyone: We fly on planes. We are your colors!

 Red Stripes: Red!

 White Stripes: White!

 Bright Stars: And blue!

Everyone: We are the flag that flies over you.

Itsy Bitsy Spider

Rhyme

The Itsy Bitsy Spider

Climbed up the water spout.

(*Fingers climb up thread*)

Down came the rain

And washed the spider out.

(*Wiggle fingers*)

Out came the sun

And dried up all the rain,

(*Arms make big circle*)

And the Itsy Bitsy Spider

Climbed up the spout again.

(*Fingers climb up thread again*)

The Ant and the Dove

Aesop's fable

One day a dove sat on the branch of a tree. It looked down at the stream. It saw an ant fall into the stream. The ant was drowning. So the dove pulled a leaf from the tree with its beak. It dropped the leaf into the stream. The ant climbed onto the leaf and floated to safety.

Later, a hunter came to the stream. The hunter saw the dove in the tree. He wanted to shoot it. When the ant saw this, it stung the hunter on the foot. The dove heard the hunter scream and flew away to safety.

If you help others, they will help you.

An Elephant Goes Like This and That

Rhyme

An elephant goes like this and that.

He's terribly big,

And he's terribly fat.

He has no fingers,

And he has no toes,

But, goodness gracious, what a nose!

Fuzzy Wuzzy Was a Bear

Rhyme

Fuzzy Wuzzy was a bear.

Fuzzy Wuzzy had no hair.

Fuzzy Wuzzy wasn't fuzzy, was he?

Was he bare?

Dinner For a Giant

Rhyme

A truck load of sausages.
A train load of peas.
A helicopter bucket full of
Chocolate chips and cheese.
A swimming pool of ice cream.
What does it make?
A dinner for a giant
And a giant tummy ache!

I Stand In the Sand

Rhyme

I stand in the sand with a ticket in my hand.

I stand in the sand and I wait.

I wait to catch a ride on the 5 o'clock whale,

But the 5 o'clock whale is late.

I Hear Thunder

Finger-Play Rhyme

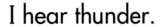

I hear thunder.

I hear thunder.

Listen, don't you?

Listen, don't you?

(*Cup hands to ears*)

Pitter, patter, raindrops.

Pitter, patter, raindrops.

(*Raise arms up and down, wriggling fingers*)

I am wet.

So are you.

(*Wipe hands down arms*)

Where Are You Going?
Play

Characters

 Storyteller *(teacher or other fluent reader)*

 Farmer

 Duck

 Sheep

 The Rooster with the Smile

 Cat

 Cow

Storyteller: One day, a farmer got on her tractor to go to the county fair. The farm animals wanted to know where she was going.

All the farm animals: Where are you going? Where? Where? Where?

Farmer: I am going on the tractor to the county fair.

Storyteller: The cat said:

Cat: Meeow!

Storyteller: The cow said:

Cow: Moo!

Storyteller: The rooster with the smile said:

Rooster with the Smile: Cock-a-doodle-doo!

Storyteller: The sheep said:

Sheep: Baaa!

Storyteller: The duck said:

Duck: Quack!

Storyteller: The farmer on the tractor said:

Farmer: Hop on the back!

Everyone: Hooray! Let's go!

One, Two, Buckle My Shoe

Counting Rhyme

One, two, buckle my shoe.

Three, four, touch the floor.

Five, six, pick up sticks.

Seven, eight, lay them straight.

Nine, ten, a big fat hen.

The Rainbow

Poem

"The sky looks sad," said little Ned's Dad,

"The rainbow looks like a frown!"

"No," said Ned, who was standing on his head.

"Look at it upside down!"

"The sky looks happy," said little Ned's Dad,

"The rainbow looks like a smile!"

"Yes," said Ned, whose face was going red.

"But I might stand up for a while."

Five Fluffy Puppies

Rhyme

Five fluffy puppies in a fluffy puppy pile,

Five fluffy puppies with a fluffy puppy smile,

Five fluffy puppies wagging tails at each other,

All in a pile with their fluffy puppy mother.

Which Way Does the Wind Blow?

Rhyme

Which way does the wind blow,

And where does it go?

It goes over the water.

It rides over the snow.

It blows and tosses

The leaves from the trees.

It blows and howls

The waves from the sea.

And where does it come from

And where does it go?

The weather vane can tell you.

The weather vane will know.

This Is My Little House

Finger-Play Rhyme

This is my little house. *(Make house with fingers)*

This is the door. *(Hands joined, palms out)*

The windows are shiny, *(Polish windows)*

And so is the floor. *(Polish floor)*

Outside there is a chimney,

As tall as can be, *(Tall, stretch hands)*

With smoke that goes curling up. *(Wave hand slowly)*

Come and see. *(Finger beckoning)*

Faster Than You

Play

Cheetah

Hello Mr. Turtle how do you do?
I'm Mr. Cheetah and I'm faster than you.

Turtle

If you think, Mr. Cheetah, you are faster than me,
Let's have a race to the coconut tree.

Cheetah

Yes let's, Mr. Turtle, if that's okay.
I'm a cheetah, I can beat a turtle any old day.

So where, Mr. Turtle, is the coconut tree?

Turtle

Out there Mr. Cheetah, on that island in the sea.

Cheetah

In the sea, Mr. Turtle? But that's not fair!
I'm a runner, Mr. Turtle. I can't swim anywhere!

Turtle

That's true, Mr. Cheetah, that's very, very true.
So I guess that makes me faster than you.

Dots and Spots

Rhyme

I've got a lot of spots on my flowerpots.

I've got a lot of dots on my spots.

How many dots on the spots on my pots?

Lots and lots and lots!

Look in the Lake

Play

Characters

 Little Green Snake

 Little Red Snake

 Little Blue Snake

 Little Yellow Snake

 Crocodile

 Everyone (everyone else in class or group)

 Everyone: Little Green Snake! Look in the lake! Tell us what you see!

 Little Green Snake: There's a little green snake! There's a little green snake like me!

 Everyone: Little Red Snake! Look in the lake! Tell us what you see!

 Little Red Snake: There's a little red snake! There's a little red snake like me!

 Everyone: Little Blue Snake! Look in the lake! Tell us what you see!

 Little Blue Snake: There's a little blue snake! There's a little blue snake like me!

 Everyone: Little Yellow Snake! Look in the lake! Tell us what you see!

 Little Yellow Snake: There's a snappy crocodile looking at me!

 Crocodile: Grrrroooaaaaaagh!

 Everyone: Little Yellow Snake! Get away from the lake!

 Little Yellow Snake: I got away! I got away! I'm a clever yellow snake. That snappy crocodile can't get me!

 Everyone: Hooray!

Ladybug, Ladybug

Jump-Rope Rhyme

Ladybug, ladybug, turn around,

Ladybug, ladybug, touch the ground.

Ladybug, ladybug, shine your shoes,

Ladybug, ladybug, read the news.

Ladybug, ladybug, how old are you?

One, two, three, four...

I Like Chasing Chickens

Poem

I like chasing chickens.

I like chasing dogs.

I like chasing kittens.

I like chasing frogs.

I like chasing chipmunks

And squirrels up a tree.

I don't like chasing crocodiles

But they like chasing me!

I Like Trucks

Opinion

I like sensible trucks that get the job done.

I like no-nonsense trucks that keep the streets
clean and take the garbage away.

I like hard-working trucks that keep the roads
open and bring food to the supermarket.

But when it comes to flashy, noisy, useless monster trucks,

I love them!

What's That?
Play

Characters

 *Leader*   *Followers*

 Leader: What's that baby dog dancing in the park?

 Followers: It's a puppy! It's a puppy! It goes bark, bark, bark!

 Leader: What's that baby horse skating in the hay?

 Followers: It's a foal! It's a foal! It goes neigh, neigh, neigh!

 Leader: What's that baby hen singing in its sleep?

 Followers: It's a chick! It's a chick! It goes cheep, cheep, cheep!

 Leader: What's that baby cow visiting the zoo?

 Followers: It's a calf! It's a calf! It goes moo, moo, moo!

 Leader: What's that baby sheep playing the guitar?

 Followers: It's a lamb! It's a lamb! It goes baa, baa, baa!

 Leader: What's that baby cat juggling with the cow?

 Followers: It's a kitten! It's a kitten! It goes meow, meow, meow!

 Leader: Who are those people making all the noise?

 Followers: It's us! It's us! Noisy girls and noisy boys!

bark, bark, bark!
cheep, cheep, cheep!
baa, baa, baa!
gh, neigh. igh!
meow, meow, meow!
moo, moo, moo!

Index